GARY JONES

Philadelphia Travel Guide

Contents

Introduction

Ben Franklin Bridge

In the United States, tourists more often go to cities like New York City and Los Angeles. However, one city should also be as visited as these major coastal cities is Philadelphia.

Why? The City of Brotherly Love not only has its own Old World charm but is also the birthplace of the United States of America.

Philly is also a cosmopolitan city with a diverse culture, owing to the influx of European immigrants like Germans, Italians, Dutch, and many others.

Independence Hall

Philadelphia has everything to offer its visitors. Here, you can enjoy local music, elite sports, museums, fantastic food, shopping opportunities, and elegant hotel accommodations at affordable rates.

The city's atmosphere is unique. You can revel in Old Town's cobblestone streets, Center City's murals, and Washington Square's relaxed vibe. Philadelphia is a welcoming city that accepts people from all walks of life.

You can spend the day visiting historical monuments like the Liberty Bell or you can go visit museums. In the late hours, you can enjoy the night at jazz bars, tapas bars, or go for a Latin American dancing adventure.

Philadelphia has it all – for the local and for the tourist.

1

Why Visit Philadelphia?

It is America's birthplace. Independence Hall is where the Declaration of Independence was signed in 1776. It is also where the Continental Congress signed the U.S. Constitution soon after the American Revolutionary War ended.

Cheesesteaks and breweries. Philly is rich with the aroma of sizzling beef, cheese, and buttery soft pretzels. After you eat some of the famed cheesesteaks and cheesesteak sandwiches, go to the local breweries and order a selection of craft beers.

One of the country's best sporting cities. Sports fans would delight in this city. Here, you can watch games featuring the 76ers (NBA), the Eagles (NFL), the Phillies (Major League Baseball, and the Flyers (NHL).

Major League Baseball

A city rich in history. Here, you can see 18th century homes, cobbled streets, and historic churches. You can explore this city on foot, especially at Old City and Center City.

Cinema and art. Philadelphia is iconic, not only for its art, but also for the Rocky Steps featured in 'Rocky,' the classic movie starring Sylvester Stallone.

WHY VISIT PHILADELPHIA?

2

Brief History and Background

John Barry statue

During the American Revolution, the city of Philadelphia was one of the most important and largest cities. Established by William Penn as a community of religious tolerance, the city's spirit helped spur the move for American Independence.

Swedes were the first European settlers, who founded a community at the Schuylkill. England also set its sights on the region. In 1681, King Charles II granted William Penn the land that soon became Pennsylvania.

From 1682, Penn and his group set up Philadelphia on the Pennsylvania colony's southeast corner, based on a set town development plan. Soon, Philadelphia attracted other immigrants from Europe. The city established trade with the West Indies and soon became the colonies' most important city. Philly became a city in 1701.

One of Philadelphia's most famous residents, the scientist Benjamin Franklin, became known for his efforts in the American Revolution. The Continental Congresses were held in the city. The British also occupied the city from September 26, 1777 to June 18, 1778. After the American Revolutionary War, the Continental Congress then drafted the U.S. Constitution.

Other cities economically prospered at a more exponential rate than Philadelphia after the American Revolution. By 1790, New York was a bigger city. Still, Philadelphia suburbs still developed during the 19th century, including the suburbs of Moyamensing, Kensington, Southwark, Northern Liberties, and Spring Gardens.

In 1876, the city hosted a major international exposition to commemorate 100 years of the Declaration of Independence. From May 10, 1876 to November 10, 1876, the expo showcased at least 50 countries' industries.

Philadelphia was and continues to be an important cultural and scientific center. Founded in 1740, the University of Penn-sylvania occupies a 120-acre campus in the western portion of the city. Founded in 1805, the Academy of Natural Science is one of the oldest scientific institutions.

Founded in 1876, the Philadelphia Museum of Art, displays numerous Impressionist art. The nation's oldest zoological garden, The Philadelphia Zoo, hosts 1,600 exotic and rare animals.

6

3

Best Time to Go and Safety

The best time to go is in the spring between March and May as the number of tourists is still relatively low and accommodation is relatively cheaper. Moreover, you can also see a burst of cherry blossoms all over the city streets and parks.

If you don't mind the bitter cold, you can go to Philly during autumn and winter. During this time, you can get hotel rates at bargain prices.

The peak season is summer. By this time, you can see a swarm of tourists at the Philadelphia Zoo, Independence Hall, and other tourist destinations.

Weather

March to May.

The temperatures during this time is still a bit chilly. March temperatures range from the mid-30s to the lower 50s, while the May temperatures range from the mid-50s to the low 70s.

However, hotel rates are nevertheless reasonable. You may bump into some school field trips, but the crowds are still manageable. One of the best places to go to during spring is Fairmount Park. Here, you can see cherry blossoms in full bloom.

June to August.

The peak season are the months of June, July, and August. Temperatures range from the lower 70s to the mid-80s, and the weather is great to enjoy the numerous outdoor events and festivals. However, hotel rates are steep, which makes the summer months an expensive time to visit Philly.

September to November.

9

Temperatures at the beginning of autumn range from the high 70s and the low 60s. By November, however, the temperature and the number of tourists drop. Hotel room rates are also becoming cheaper.

If you love to see Philadelphia in autumn, you can go to Independence Hall, Benjamin Franklin Freeway, Wissahickon Valley Park, and Fairmount Park. At these places, you can see the leaves change from the summer greens to the autumn yellows and reds.

December to February.

Winter is an affordable time to visit Philly. However, the temperatures can be freezing with averages of the mid-20s.

The chilly weather still encourages residents and visitors to enjoy winter activities covering various outdoor and indoor events. Some of these festivals include the Blue Cross RiverRink Winterfest and a number of holiday light shows.

Safety in the City

The City of Brotherly Love is generally safe, particularly the tourist-heavy areas like Center City. However, repeat travelers to the city would tell you to be careful when venturing to other parts of Philadelphia like West Philly or South Philly.

As a responsible tourist, it's essential to use common sense. At all times, keep valuables in check. Hide them if you can. If you're not sure about going to a certain destination, drive or get a cab, particularly at night.

4

Getting Around Philadelphia

Philadelphia's transportation infrastructure is advanced, making it an inspiration for newer cities. These cities are spending billions of dollars to have systems that can cater to larger populations and are also as cutting-edge as Philly's transport system.

Philadelphia International Airport caters to 32 million passengers annually. For the Amtrak train network, ridership increased 3.3% from 2006 to 2007 with 3.7 million riders arriving and boarding at 30th Street Station along the Northeast Corridor.

Philly also has 2 interstate highways, seven rail lines (regional), 41 regional and local bus lines, 5 trolley lines, more than 150 bicycle lanes, and a high-speed line going to New Jersey.

About 40% of Center City residents walk to and from work. Zip and Philly CarShare, which are ride-sharing companies, allow residents to choose not to own vehicles.

Getting Around Philadelphia

To explore Philadelphia, hop on a Phlash bus or tour the city on foot. Some attractions, like the Philadelphia Zoo, call for you to ride some sort of transport. However, many of the city's attractions are located at pedestrian-friendly neighborhoods like Society Hill, Rittenhouse Square, and Old City.

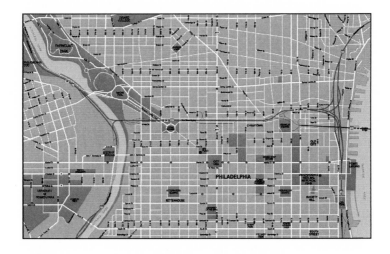

To get from the airport and go around the city, you can use the system of buses, subways, and trolleys. A cab ride to Center City from the airport costs $28.50. During the months of March to December, you can access the city via the purple Phlash buses.

You can use ride-sharing services like Lyft or Uber, since taxi rides can become expensive, especially when the number of trips and the fares add up. If you're bringing your own vehicle to Philly, get a good map and be prepared for parking and driving frustrations.

From a nearby city going to Philadelphia, take the Amtrak. If you're from New York, you can take a New Jersey Transit-SEPTA (Southeast Pennsylvania Transportation Authority) train combination.

SEPTA Phone: (215) 580-7800

5

Top 5 Affordable Hotels

Philadelphia – the City of Brotherly Love – is where you want to be to learn more about the United States of America's early history. Philadelphia is more than just a historical treasure. You'd appreciate the culinary scene and enjoy baseball games at Citizens Bank Park featuring the Philadelphia Phillies.

Before you enjoy your Philly vacation, book a safe accommodation that suits your needs. Below are some of the best, affordable 4- and 3-star hotels and suites that you can consider for your vacation and historical escapade.

The Windsor Suites Philadelphia

Located at 1700 Benjamin Franklin Parkway, The Windsor Suites Philadelphia's accommodations feature well-equipped kitchens, which include a refrigerator, dishwasher, and stove. Suites come with complimentary Wi-Fi and flat-screen TVs with cable channels.

The hotel is located just 484 meters away from 15th Street Trolley Station and 645 meters away from The Barnes Foundation and the City Hall Subway Station.

Whenever you don't feel like preparing your own meals, you can dine at any of the hotel's restaurants that feature a variety of International cuisines. Asia on the Parkway serves Thai and Chinese cuisines daily for dinner and lunch.

If you want more traditional and familiar fare, dine at the Irish-inspired Con Murphy's, a pub that serves American and Irish dishes for breakfast, lunch, and dinner.

The 4-star Windsor Suites Philadelphia is rated well by customers for its accessibility to the airport, which is 9.9 miles (15.9km) away. The 30th Street Amtrak is also 1 mile (1.6km) away.

Couples especially like the hotel. Guests also get more value for what they paid for as compared to other Philly hotel properties.

Phone: +1 215-981-5678

Wyndham Philadelphia – Historic District

Located at 400 Arch Street, Wyndham Philadelphia – Historic District's accommodations feature an onsite restaurant and a rooftop pool that opens during the favorable months. Each room offers complimentary toiletries, a work desk, flat-screen TV, and free Wi-Fi.

The property is 645 meters away from Independence Hall, 484 meters from Liberty Bell, 2 miles (3.2km) away from 30th Street Amtrak Station, and 8.1 miles (13km) away from the Philadelphia International Airport.

If you want to be more adventurous and not avail of room service, you can dine at Coin's Restaurant & Pub and enjoy traditional American classics.

The 4-star Wyndham Philadelphia – Historic District is rated highly for its location.

Phone:+1 215-923-8660

Aloft Philadelphia Downtown

Located at 101 North Broad Street, Aloft Philadelphia Downtown's amenities include free Wi-Fi, flat-screen TV, a desk, and complimentary toiletries. The hotel also offers guests a meeting space, a bar, and a fitness center.

The structure housing the hotel is a 1920s Liberty Title building. When you enter the property, you are treated to a spectacular entrance lobby with high ceilings. You can dine at Refuel by Aloft, 24/7, which serves light meals.

The hotel is 325 meters away from the Pennsylvania Convention Center, 500 meters away from Reading Terminal Market and Philadelphia City Hall, and 1 mile (1.6km) away from Liberty Bell and Independence Hall.

Guests, especially couples, rate the 3-star Aloft Philadelphia Downtown highly for its close proximity to important tourist attractions. Guests also get value for money as compared to other Philly hotels.

Phone: +1 215-607-2020

DoubleTree by Hilton Philadelphia Center City

Located at 237 South Broad Street, DoubleTree by Hilton Philadelphia Center City has room amenities like a radio and pay-per-view. The hotel also offers video games, ironing facilities, a hairdryer, a fitness center, and an indoor pool.

The hotel is 966 meters away from the Pennsylvanian Convention Center, 900 meters away from Liberty Bell, 0.6 mile (965 meters) from Reading Terminal Market, and 3.4 miles (5.47km) away from the Philadelphia Zoo.

For dining, the hotel has its Balcony Restaurant that offers a-la-carte or buffet breakfast. Another dining option at the hotel is the Standing O Restaurant, which is a bar and a bistro.

The 3-star DoubleTree by Hilton Philadelphia Center City is rated highly by guests for its restaurants as well as its location.

Phone: +1 215-893-1600

Hampton Inn Philadelphia Center City – Convention Center

Located at 1301 Race Street, Hampton Inn Philadelphia Center City – Convention Center offers guests complimentary Wi-Fi and daily breakfast. Each room has a private bathroom, a work desk, and flat-screen TV that shows cable channels. You can get a microwave and refrigerator upon request.

The hotel is 322 meters away from the Pennsylvania Convention Center, 484 meters away from Reading Terminal Market, and 1 mile (1.6km) away from Independence Hall. The Philadelphia International Airport is 11 miles (17.7km) away.

If you want to get fit while on vacation, go to the hotel's fitness center. The onsite lounge and bar, Pub 1301, opens daily from 5:00pm to 11:00pm.

The 3-star Hampton Inn Philadelphia Center City – Convention Center is rated highly for its location as well as value for money.

Phone:+1 215-665-9100

Philadelphia Downtown

6

Top 5 Restaurants

Philadelphia is not only the place where the United States of America was born. It's also a place where you can enjoy diverse culinary experiences. Philly's reputation as a premier dining and food destination is well-known.

Restaurants all over Philly are documented in national magazines and newspapers like Food & Wine, Bon Appetit, The Washington Post, The New York Times, GQ, and others.

Choosing where to dine in Philadelphia can be a bit overwhelming, given the number of restaurants in the city. Here are some of the most-booked restaurants in the city, and these restaurants' offerings would surely not disappoint.

Parc

There's a slice of Paris in Philadelphia that's called Parc, which is a popular bistro located at Rittenhouse Square. Parc's French bistro experience lets customers enjoy a Parisian atmosphere with a beautiful sidewalk seating that overlooks Rittenhouse Square. The bistro is also one of the city's best places for alfresco dining and drinking.

As you enter the bistro's front room, you're instantly greeted by the wafting aroma of fresh-baked bread. The dining room is a more elegant affair, yet casual enough to maintain the emotion and energy of a vibrant brasserie.

Address: 227 S 18th St, Philadelphia
Web: parc-restaurant.com
Tel. No.: 215-545-2262

Talula's Garden and Talula's Daily

If you want some farm-to-table fare while visiting Philadelphia, go to Talula's Garden and Talula's Daily, which are two adjoining restaurants located in the city's Washington Square West neighborhood. Owned by Aimee Olexy and Stephen Starr, the two restaurants serve excellent cheese, homemade bread, and local ingredients.

Talula's Garden features outdoor and indoor dining rooms – lavished in greenery and color – that flow seamlessly. The restaurant serves sit-down brunch and dinner. For dinner, you can order charcuterie and cheese boards, pastas, and seasonal salads.

At Talula's Garden, you can also order oregano-infused fettuccini with ricotta and tomatoes, chocolate tahini mousse, or cauliflower cobbler with breadcrumbs and Mornay sauce. The wine list is impressive as are the unique cocktails added with unusual ingredients like cherry blossoms and peas.

On the other hand, Talula's Daily caters to clientele who come for homemade muffins, morning espressos, charcuterie, lunchtime salads and sandwiches, gourmet foodstuff, and gift items.

At night, Talula's Daily assumes a dining room setting with a seasonal menu. Costing $55, the five-course dinner can include dishes like duck cassoulet, salmon rillettes, hazelnut profiteroles, or triple crème cheeses. You can pair your dinner with cider, wine, or beer.

Address: 210 W Washington Square, Philadelphia, PA 19106 (Garden)
Address: 208 W Washington Square, Philadelphia, PA 19106 (Daily)

Web: talulasgarden.com, talulasdaily.com
Tel. No.: 215-592-7787 (Talula's Garden)
Tel. No.: 215-592-6555 (Talula's Daily)

The Love

Located at Rittenhouse Square, The Love features American fare with seasonal, fresh food. Aimee Olexy and Stephen Starr's two-level restaurant serves upscale fare in a swanky yet affordable space that's bathed in natural sunlight.

The starters are something you have try. Highly recom-mended is the cheese plate with eight types of American cheeses dressed with bread, spreads, and berries. The Saturday and Sunday brunch features truffle scrambled eggs and shrimp and grits.

Address: 130 S 18th St, Philadelphia, PA 19103
Web: theloverestaurant.com
Tel. No.: 215-433-1555

Harp & Crown

Chef Michael Schulson's Harp and Crown venture lends a timeless atmosphere. Some of the featured dishes here are seasonal fare, small plates, and charcuterie. There's even a 2-lane bowling alley that's reservation-only.

Located at Rittenhouse Square, Harp and Crown features exposed brick, high ceilings, tufted booths, vintage portraits, and a wrap-around bar. The vibrant atmosphere may be reason enough to bring you here, but the entrees are what truly make this place shine.

You'll also be delighted with the weekend all-you-can-eat brunch. Cheese plates and charcuterie mix well with lamb meatballs and Spanish octopus. The spinach pesto farro pasta and the steaks are some of the most satisfying dishes that you can order at Harp and Crown.

Address: 1525 Sansom St, Philadelphia, PA 19102

Web: harpcrown.com
Tel. No.: 215-330-2800

Mad Rex

Located at the Northern Liberties neighborhood, Mad Rex is a post-apocalyptic-themed restaurant and bar that has a virtual reality lounge. At Mad Rex, you'll find post-apocalyptic objects like cargo nets, barbed wire, graffiti, a helicopter model, bats, axes, and fake guns.

At the virtual reality lounge, you can journey through your selected experience and you get VR goggles too. Mad Rex is just across SugarHouse Casino.

While the food at Mad Rex is delicious, the interiors offer a whole other experience. At the restaurant, you can enjoy plenty of bar staples like salads, flatbreads, and more expensive food items like seafood and steaks cooked and flavored with Himalayan salt.

Address: 1000 Frankford Ave #1, Philadelphia, PA 19125
Web: themadrex.com
Tel. No.: 267-773-7566

7

Best Famous Landmarks in the City

Not only is Philadelphia one of America's major cities, it's also known as the country's birthplace. Thus, it's only fitting that its most famous landmarks are American Independence-related.

There are so many historical and modern landmarks in Philadelphia, which is why it gets around 42 million visitors a year. The city's landscape is an eclectic mix of the old and the new.

Contemporary office buildings are now built along Independence National Historic Park's cobblestone streets. Additionally, the park is home to historic sights and buildings that include Independence Hall, Franklin Court, and Liberty Bell.

Society Hill – in the city's south – is Philly's original residential district. Here, 18th century buildings have been restored to perfection. Northwest Philadelphia's Germantown is also an older residential area once populated by Dutch and Germans.

Along Schuylkill River, to the west, is Fairmount Park, which is a green expanse with Federal-style mansions, as well as the Rodin Museum and the Philadelphia Museum of Art. Further south is the museum district, which contains the Academy of Natural Sciences and the Franklin Institute of Science Museum.

Fairmount Park

If you want to venture outside the city limits, you can go to Peddler's Village, a colonial-style town that's one hour away from Center City. With seasonal festivals, a 71-room inn, the Giggleberry Fair that would appeal to kids, and stores for a variety of shoppers, it's astounding how this small town can attract tourists by the millions.

Philadelphia has so many attractions, which can't be covered in just a three-day visit. You need to visit Philly continually to be able to explore the city's offerings. Below are some of the famous city attractions that are worth looking into on your first visit to the city.

Independence National Historical Park

The Independence National Historic Park (INHP) stands on the site of American democracy's birthplace. The INHP houses over two dozen historically significant places, with some of the more famous being the Independence Hall and Liberty Bell Pavilion.

Open to the public all year and normally with free admission, these culturally- and historically-significant sites include banks, a home of a former First Lady, and cemeteries that serve as resting places for some of the United States' prominent early citizens.

Some significant sites at INHP include: Congress Hall, West Wing, Old City Hall, The President's House, Benjamin Franklin Museum, 318 Market Street, Printing Office, Franklin Court, and National Constitution Center.

Other sites are Christ Church and Christ Church Burial Ground, Carpenter's Hall, Tomb of the Unknown Soldier of the American Revolution, Washington Square, Welcome Park, Declaration (Graff) House, and City Tavern.

Benjamin Franklin Museum

Other INHP sites include: First Bank of the United States, Second Bank of the United States, Dolley Todd (Madison) House, The Bishop White House, American Philosophical Society Museum, Thomas Bond House, and Free Quaker Meeting House.

Other sites are Mikveh Israel Cemetery, Old St. Joseph's Catholic Church, Merchants' Exchange Building, New Hall Military Museum, Magnolia Garden, and Rose Garden.

Independence Hall is flanked by Congress Hall, where the United States of America's first Congress met during 1790-1800 and where John Adams and George Washington were elected presidents. Old City Hall was not exactly the town hall, but was the Supreme Court's seat during 1791-1800.

The Independence Mall, north of the Independence Hall, was laid out in 1948. Off Dock Street, the Visitor Center is an excellent place to start the day. At the center, you can get tickets, current information, and maps for walking tours.

Address: 143 S. 3rd Street Philadelphia, PA 19106
Web: https://www.nps.gov/inde/index.htm
Tel. No.: 215-965-2305

Philadelphia Zoo

If you want to take a breather from American history, go visit the Philadelphia Zoo with your family. As one of the best laid-out zoos, the Philadelphia Zoo is nestled within a 42-acre Victorian garden with formal shrubbery, animal sculptures, and tree-lined walks.

The Philadelphia Zoo has so many firsts that it should be impossible for you to miss this. In 1859, the zoo became the country's first chartered zoo. In 1928, the zoo became the first American zoo to witness the first chimp and orangutan births. In 1993, the zoo became the first U.S. zoo to exhibit white lions.

Aside from the roughly 1,600 animal residents, the Philadelphia Zoo is known for its historic buildings including William Penn's grandson's country home, a 500-plant species botanical collection, fine veterinary facilities, and cutting-edge research facilities.

The zoo also has its pioneering Zoo360 program, which offers innovations like an animal travel exploration trail system. The see-through mesh trails allow animals more room to move about the zoo premises. Through the Zoo360 initiative, you can see orangutans, lemurs, tigers, and other animals in near-natural environments.

Other Philadelphia Zoo initiatives and attractions include the McNeil Aviation Center, Big Cat Falls, PECO Primate Reserve, and KidZooU, among others.

You can get tickets to the Philadelphia Zoo, which is open year-round and all day, online or at the gate. If you're bringing transportation, the zoo offers ample open parking space as well as a 4-floor parking garage.

You can also access the zoo through public transport. SEPTA serves the zoo with train routes and buses stopping within blocks of the tourist attraction. When in season, you can also reach the zoo through the Phlash shuttle.

Address: 3400 W Girard Ave, Philadelphia, PA 19104
Web: philadelphiazoo.org
Tel. No.: 215-243-1100

Independence Hall

Independence Hall, which is located within the Independence National Historical Park premises, was once the State House of the Colony of Pennsylvania.

However, it's more known as the location where the Continental Congress adopted the Declaration of Independence on July 4, 1776. Eleven years later, the Continental Congress again met here and wrote the U.S. Constitution.

Independence Hall

In the Assembly Hall, the attraction's highlight, the Second Continental Congress discussed their intent to gain independence from Britain. The Assembly Hall was where they signed the Declaration and where they elected George Washington as the Continental Army's Commander-in-Chief.

National Park rangers conduct guided tours that start in the courtroom where lawyers from both sides shared law books and tables. Moreover, dominating the Assembly Hall is the 'rising sun' chair of George Washington.

In the West Wing next door, the inkstand used during the Declaration of Independence signing as well as the Constitution's original draft are displayed prominently.

Independence Hall is just across the Liberty Bell Pavilion. While you don't pay for the entrance, tickets are limited and visits are timed, and you should be ready for security screenings.

During the peak months of March to December, you'll be needing the tickets to enter. After 5:00pm, at all times, you can freely enter. You also don't need a ticket to enter during January and February, Thanksgiving Day, Christmas Eve, or Independence Day.

Address: 520 Chestnut St, Philadelphia, PA 19106
    Web: https://www.nps.gov/inde/planyourvisit/indepen-
dencehall.htm

Tel. No.: 215-965-2305

Please Touch Museum

At the Please Touch Museum, your kids get to dictate the terms. As one of the country's top museums for children, Please Touch Museum offers families and children interactive learning experiences across over 60,000 square feet of exhibits at the Memorial Hall's Fairmount Park.

The interactive museum encourages children to learn in a fun way. It also gives them the opportunity to explore fantasy worlds, history, space, and the whole wide world.

Since 1976, the Museum has been bringing together the past, present, and future via interactive exhibit zones within 157,000 square feet. There are also four areas dedicated for children 3 years old and younger.

Families can also ride the perfectly restored Woodside Park Dentzel Carousel, originally made in Philadelphia in 1908. Stored for over 40 years, the carousel is now housed in its dedicated 9,000 sq. ft. glass pavilion at the Memorial Hall's east side.

While many museums in the city have dedicated children's corners, Please Touch Museum is a kid-dominated place that also houses the 'Centennial Exploration' exhibit, which explores the 1876 Centennial Exhibition and the Memorial Hall's history.

At the Please Touch Museum, children can 'drive' an actual bus and sail a boat on a small Delaware River recreation. At Nature's Pond, young children can see animals set in a lily pond as well as within high grass.

At the Fairytale Garden, children can also enjoy nursery rhymes and stories. At the Supermarket, children get to work as they stock shelves with plastic produce and popular products, load their carts, and pay for their orders.

The River Adventures exhibit lets children learn about physics and science by using waterwheels, dams, locks, levers, and other equipment that manipulate water.

If possible, avoid the Please Touch Museum during the rainy days. Mornings are busy with the many school group tours around. The best times to visit the Museum are on Mondays (groups are not usually scheduled during this time) and during the afternoons. It's also recommended to buy entrance tickets in advance.

Address: 4231 Avenue of the Republic, Philadelphia, PA 19131
Web: pleastouchmuseum.org
Tel. No.: 215-581-3181

Liberty Bell Pavilion

For a long time now, the Liberty Bell symbolizes independence and freedom in the United States. The Bell can be viewed in the Liberty Bell Pavilion, which also contains videos and exhibits about the Bell's history.

Liberty Bell

In the late 19th century, the Bell was toured around the country to conquer divisions left over by the Civil War as well as bring up a sense of freedom among the people. In 1916, the Bell ended its journey in Philadelphia.

The Liberty Bell is worth a visit as it's one of the world's most recognizable freedom symbols. At the Liberty Bell Pavilion, guests can see and experience the Bell up close. The Pavilion's quieter alcoves allow visitors to see a brief History Channel film that traces how suffragists, abolitionists, and other groups considered the Bell as their freedom symbol.

Here, you can view X-rays of the Bell's inner workings, particularly the Bell's crack. There are exhibitions of the Bell's image found in items like wind chimes to ice cream molds.

The Pavilion's majestic glass walls offer powerful and dramatic views of the Bell. Through the glass, you can see the Independence Hall in the background. You can enter the Liberty Bell Pavilion without fees or tickets. However, be aware that there are long lines during the busy tourist seasons.

Address: N 6th St & Market St, Philadelphia, PA 19106
Web: https://www.nps.gov/inde/learn/
historyculture/stories-libertybell.htm
Tel. No.: 215-965-2305

8

Best Museums

When you visit Philadelphia, you can't miss any of its museums. Fortunately, the city boasts of a diverse museum scene, with topics for all interests and ages. Some museums take a day to explore, others you need to take multiple visits to explore, while other museums you can experience in just a few hours.

You can visit any museum alone, or go with a group, with family and friends. See the history of Philadelphia or witness the vibrant art collection. Whichever museum you visit, you're always in for a treat.

Museum of the American Revolution

If you want to experience the events that led to the birth of the United States of America, visit the Museum of the American Revolution. Just opened in 2017, the Museum guides you on an immersive and comprehensive tour through American history's most important event – its independence from Britain.

At the Museum, you'll witness realistic military reenactments, huge Liberty Tree recreations, battle exhibitions, an 18th century privateer ship, opening shots, and a collection of art installations, weapons, and books. Your visit's highlight is a short film followed by a glimpse of the George Washington's war tent.

The Museum opens daily from 10:00am to 5:00pm. Entrance costs $19 and is valid for 2 successive days. If you want Guided Highlight or Early Access tours, pay a bit more.

Address: 101 S 3rd St, Philadelphia, PA 19106
Web: amrevmuseum.org
Tel. No.: 215-253-6731

Eastern State Penitentiary

If you're feeling adventurous and want to see another side of Philadelphia, go visit the Eastern State Penitentiary. Built during the 19th century, the prison was once one of the world's most notorious and expensive prisons.

Eastern State Penitentiary

The penitentiary is no longer used and is now in ruins. Even a few groups fascinated with the supernatural claim the prison is actually haunted.

First used in 1829, the prison was the first facility to attempt to reform prisoners through strict isolation. Some of the more notorious crooks like Al Capone and Slick Willie Sutton were imprisoned here.

Al Capone's Cell

You can participate in day tours – complete with hands-on or audio history guides and art installations – that cover the cell blocks. If you love a touch of spookiness, visit the penitentiary at Halloween and witness the 'Terror Behind the Walls.' The prison then becomes a terrifying and massive haunted house with shock therapy, carnage, and zombie inmates.

You can buy online tickets for the popular 'Terror Behind the Walls' beginning May. The prison is open to visitors every day from 10:00am to 5:00pm. Entrance is $14, and wear closed-toe yet comfortable footwear.

Address: 2027 Fairmount Ave, Philadelphia, PA 19130
Web: easternstate.org
Tel. No.: 215-236-3300

National Museum of American Jewish History

Many major American cities have significant Jewish populations, the city of Philadelphia included. One such place documenting the Jewish community's history is the National Museum of American Jewish History, which is a Smithsonian Institute affiliate.

Nestled in the historic district, the Museum highlights the country's history through a Jewish-American perspective. In the stunning, 4-floor contemporary building, you're invited to begin the historical journey from the top floor, and working all the way down.

National Museum of American Jewish History

Through your journey, you get to explore Jews' experience that goes beyond the Holocaust. You'll learn about American Jews' immigration history, triumphs, and modern issues through compelling artwork, religious artifacts, and interactive exhibits.

You may also want to drop by the gift shop to see what souvenirs you can bring home. The Museum opens Tuesdays to Fridays from 10:00am to 5:00pm, and Saturdays and Sundays from 10:00am to 5:30pm. Entrance is $15. The Museum is closed on certain Jewish holidays and on most federal holidays.

Address: 101 S Independence Mall E, Philadelphia, PA 19106
Web: nmajh.org
Tel. No.: 215-923-3811

Mütter Museum

As a branch of The College of Physicians of Philadelphia, the Mütter Museum is not your average museum. Sure, it's a science museum, but what it features is out of the ordinary.

The Museum, which specializes in medical peculiarities, exhibits oddities and human remains like conjoined twins liver(s), Albert Einstein's brain (just a normal-sized brain), and some 139 human skulls.

Also among the 25,000-strong collection are skeletal and wet human model specimens, balloon-sized testicles, and unusual medical apparatus. Also on exhibition are a vertebra from John Wilkes Booth's body and the jaw tumor of William Howard Taft.

Check out the Civil War Medicine exhibit, where you'll learn why and how the sick and wounded found their way to Philadelphia. With an $18 admission, the Museum opens daily from 10:00am to 5:00pm. On Mondays and Tuesdays, walk-ins are treated to a $2 discount.

Address: 19 S 22nd St, Philadelphia, PA 19103
Web: muttermuseum.org
Tel. No.: 215-560-8564

Franklin Institute

If you're traveling with your family, check out the Franklin Institute. Here, your five senses are entertained with a lot of hands-on playing and learning.

Franklin Institute

Spend an entire day doing activities like riding in a 350-ton Baldwin steam train, stargazing inside the planetarium, making puzzles, flying in a Blue Angels flight simulator, observing a cow's eye's dissection, or watching a light show at the Franklin Memorial.

You may also want to join some of the Institute's special events that vary throughout the year. The Institute opens daily from 9:30am to 5:00pm.

During special events from Thursdays to Saturdays, last entry is at 6:30pm.

Institute members enjoy free admission. For non-members, tickets for children are at $19 and adults' are at $23. Tickets for escape room and special exhibits are not part of general admission, so buy tickets for such exhibits beforehand.

Address: 222 N 20th St, Philadelphia, PA 19103
Web: fi.edu
Tel. No.: 215-448-1200

9

Best Art Galleries

Philadelphia is a hotspot for traditional, contemporary, and eclectic art. The city features an array of traditional, eclectic, and unique galleries that cater to your artistic fancy, whether you're into period art or contemporary art.

The best of Philadelphia's art galleries make art accessible to everyone, supporting the city's burgeoning arts community and making sure art lovers are appeased.

Philadelphia Museum of Art

Established in 1876, the Philadelphia Museum of Art continues to be one of the country's most impressive and largest galleries. Its majestic architecture, which reminds of ancient Greek temples, is itself a worthy masterpiece.

Philadelphia Museum of Art

The Museum's 240,000-piece collection boasts of Renaissance and contemporary treasures. There's also a sculpture garden as well as over 80 period rooms. You should also visit the Asian teahouses, the Art Deco building, as a well as a room dedicated to renowned Philadelphian Thomas Eakins.

If you're a local, you're lucky. If you're visiting the Museum, avail of the consecutive 2-day ticket. End your tour with a run and have your photo taken on the Rocky Steps.

Rocky Steps

The Museum opens from Tuesdays to Sundays from 10:00am to 5:00pm. However, the main building is open until 8:45pm during Wednesdays and Fridays, when you can savor in appetizers and cocktails.

If you don't like to pay the standard $20 fee, you can visit during every month's first Sunday and each Wednesday from 5:00pm to closing, where you 'pay what you wish.'

Address: 2600 Benjamin Franklin Pkwy, Philadelphia, PA 19130
Web: philamuseum.org
Tel. No.: 215-763-8100

Barnes Foundation

If you're a lover of French Impressionist art and Paris seems like a million miles away, just head over to the Barnes Foundation. The Spring Garden setting boasts of an exciting collection, including 69 Paul Cezanne works. Other artists featured in this collection include Henri Matisse, Pierre-Auguste Renoir, Edgar Degas, Pablo Picasso, and early modern African art.

Albert Barnes made people see art in the perspective of visual experiences. Instead of genre and region, the museum is arranged uniquely by aesthetic concepts of lines, color, and light. Thus, it's best to come on a warm and sunny day, when you can also experience the majestic landscape.

The Barnes Foundation opens on Wednesdays to Mondays from 11:00am to 5:00pm, but it's not open on Tuesdays. If you want skip the regular $25 admission fee, you can go there for free during the first Sunday of each month.

At each month's first Friday, enjoy after-hours cocktails, live music, and special exhibits and talks. The Barnes Foundation is close to the SEPTA train line.

Address: 2025 Benjamin Franklin Pkwy, Philadelphia, PA 19130
Web: barnesfoundation.org
Tel. No.: 215-278-7000

The Clay Studio

The Clay Studio is located at 139 N Second St. The world-renowned venue for contemporary ceramics is also an exhibition space, ceramics studio, and community-oriented education center. Since 1974, the Studio has been promoting ceramic arts, as well as making clay a tactile, accessible medium for the community.

Since 1979, the Studio has been an officially-designated non-profit educational institute and has helped greatly to revitalize the Old City's gallery district.

The Studio is known for its diverse exhibition and educational programs and has become the focus for ceramic arts. The Studio has hosted major international exhibitions like 2001's British Studio Ceramics, 2003's Chinese Ceramics Today, and 2006's From the North: Canadian Ceramics.

The Clay Studio is always committed to the community through working with artists, regional cultural institutions, and community and school centers.

Address: 139 N 2nd St, Philadelphia, PA 19106
Web: theclaystudio.org
Tel. No.: 215-925-3453

The Philadelphia Art Alliance

The Philadelphia Art Alliance (PAA) is Philadelphia's go-to place for contemporary design and craft. Here, you are treated to various presentations and exhibits of theater, music, sculpture, and painting.

Located at 251 S 18th St, the center was established in 1915 by Christine Wetherill Stevenson, a philanthropist. The center met the local arts community's need for a gallery specifically dedicated to design and craft.

The PAA, throughout the years, has been hosting 12 exhibits a year by artists that include Horace Pippin, Mary Cassatt, Man Ray, Antonio Gaudi, Gils Bakker, The Miss Rockaway Armada, and Candy DePew.

The exhibitions are usually accompanied with concerts, artist talks, workshops, concerts, performances, and readings, all of which allow visitors to engage in the disciplines of design and craft in interesting ways.

Address: 251 S 18th St, Philadelphia, PA 19103
Web: philartalliance.org
Tel. No.: 215-545-4302

Snyderman-Works Gallery

Snyderman-Works Gallery, which is located at 303 Cherry St, is a merger of two separate galleries – Snyderman Gallery established in 1983 and The Works Gallery established in 1965.

Both renowned galleries specialized in contemporary studio crafts, with Snyderman focusing on sculptural glass and studio furniture, while The Works focused on jewelry, fiber, and ceramic arts.

The galleries separately became recognized for exhibits in the 1980s, featuring works by Robert Venturi and Ettore Sottass.

In 1992, the two galleries joined forces and have since delved into other media like print, painting, sculpture, and photography. The resulting Snyderman-Works Gallery has also hosted group and solo exhibitions of artists like William Morris, Dale Chihuly, Tom Patti, Harvey Littleton, and Toots Zynsky.

The Gallery has also started numerous collaborative projects with the artists it represents to make site-specific installations. Snyderman-Works Gallery is also active in the Philadelphia arts community.

Address: 303 Cherry St, Philadelphia, PA 19106
Web: snyderman-works.com
Tel. No.: 215-238-9576

10

Best Coffee Shops

This list of the best coffee shops is composed of local coffee shops. As such, you won't find any Starbucks or Seattle's Best here as they're not exactly true-blue Philadelphian.

For many people, coffee is not only drunk to make them alert, it's also drunk as an indulgence or a luxury. If you drink coffee for its complexity and taste, and not for the caffeine, you tend to be more discriminate about the entire coffee-making process.

The best coffee shops, especially the independently-owned ones, are particular about the process from bean selection to how the final product is roasted.

Unless you're in Italy or in Morocco, wherein drinking coffee is always a go-to pastime for a tourist, you may tend to skip going into a Philly coffee shop. After all, there are other sights and attractions to visit and you want to spend the most of your vacation absorbing the Philadelphian culture.

If you do need to go inside a coffee shop, whether to relax a bit or meet up with local friends, why not go inside a homegrown one? Below are some of the best locally owned coffee shops in Philly that are worth a visit.

Old City Coffee

Located at 221 Church St, Old City Coffee boasts of an in-house roaster, ensuring that the coffee you're served is fresh. Aside from its tea and coffee menu, the café also serve light snacks, especially the Jewish Apple Cake that makes you want to order more.

Established in 1984, Old City Coffee is one of the neighborhood's most-visited places. While the place isn't large, people have been coming here for decades. The coffee shop also has a stall at Reading Terminal Market.

Web: oldcitycoffee.com
Tel. No.: 215-629-9292

Function Coffee Labs

'Where Coffee Meets Science' is the tagline for the charming, locally-grown Function Coffee Labs, which is located at 1001 S 10th St. The coffee beans' unique flavors are because they're sourced from various locations, and their offerings are sustainable.

If you want to drink what locals call the 'best black cup of coffee' in the city, come to Function Coffee Labs. The coffee shop also offers an ever-changing Laboratory Line as well as the 'House Coffee.'

To bring out the best flavor, add milk or drink your coffee black. Function Coffee Labs is also known for its 'Coffee Shot.'

Web: functioncoffeelabs.com
Tel. No.: 267-606-6734

Reanimator Coffee

If you feel tired after a long day, go to Reanimator Coffee to recharge. Located at 310 West Master Avenue, the coffee shop also hires true baristas who create 'café art' and not just serve brewed coffee.

The café has a huge open area that's busy but still lets you sit down and enjoy that cup of coffee in peace. There's also another Reanimator branch at Fishtown. Wherever you go, you're sure to drink coffee that's made the way you like it. Reanimator Coffee roasts its own beans and you can even buy bags of beans from the café as well.

Web: reanimator.com
Tel. No.: 267-758-6264

Grindcore House

Located at 1515 South 4th St, Grindcore House is where you want to enjoy eclectic interiors together with your cup of coffee. All 'heavy metal' stuff are here at the dog-loving café together with vegan lifestyle elements. You'll find the café has a bit of an 'activist attitude.'

Like many local cafes, Grindcore House grinds its own fair-trade coffee. Some of the café's offerings include non-dairy selections, syrups like coconut and marshmallow, and locally sourced food. Its 'cream cheeses' are vegan and customers love the Ghost Pepper, Pumpkin, and Jalapeño selections.

Web: grindcorehouse.com
Tel. No.: 215-839-3333

Nook Bakery and Coffee Bar

Located at 15 S. 20th St in the famous Rittenhouse Square neighborhood, Nook Bakery and Coffee Bar is a small café that's big on offering bakery products.

The café's goal is to pair freshly-roasted coffee with their in-house bakery goods like the combination of Ethiopian drip coffee with pastries or Berry Muffin.

Keeping sustainability in mind, Nook Bakery and Coffee Bar is where you want to go if you want stay away from big-name, overcrowded cafes. The café also serves lunch and breakfast.

Web: nookbakeryandcoffee.com

Tel. No.: 215-496-9033

11

Top 5 Bars

The bar culture in Philadelphia has come a long way, ever since the day when Brewerytown was just a rugged hub of fun and drink. Now, the Philadelphia bar culture has expanded to fashionable and glitzy spots around town.

The Philadelphia bar scene, which encompasses breweries, outdoor bars, rooftop bars, and fancy establishments, pours out a range of trendy and inventive craft cocktails, beer, and excellent wines. Some of the best bars and breweries are listed below.

a.bar

The 2018 Time Out Philadelphia Bar Awards recipient for the Most Creative Drinks list is a.bar, which is nested in the Rittenhouse neighborhood. This contemporary bar is a fashionable place for a fancy cocktail after work.

Grab a seat at any of the booths, the bar, or at the high tops along the periphery. Go through a creative ever-changing cocktail list that features fresh ingredients like cold-pressed juices (like carrot juice), hibiscus, and herbs.

One of a.bar's unique offerings include the 'Lucy I'm Home' cocktail, which is mixed with Aperol, Beefeater, St. Germain, lemon, ginger, and orange blossom water. If you want to keep things simple, go for a cider or beer in cans or in draft, various Amari selections, and wine as well.

Address: 1737 Walnut Street NE Corner
Web: akitchenandbar.com
Tel. No.: 215-825-7035

Oscar's Tavern

Located at Center City, Oscar's Tavern is where you want to be if you don't want to enjoy nearby Rittenhouse Square's glitzy wine dens and cocktail lounges. At Oscar's Tavern, you can enjoy pub grub, affordable beers, and friendly wait staff.

Opened in 1972, the tavern has a diner-like atmosphere with bar stools, red-vinyl booths, and wood-paneled walls. This bar does tend to fill up quickly after work hours. At the back, you'll find single-stall bathrooms, tables, and a jukebox playing nostalgic tunes.

If you're here to sample the beers, you can get familiar offerings like PBR, Yuengling, and Rolling Rock that cost from $4 to $5. When it comes to cocktails, you can enjoy martini, gin and tonic, Screwdriver, and Long Island iced tea.

Not only can you enjoy cocktails here, you can also enjoy culinary fare like chicken fingers, cheesesteaks, burgers, cheese fries, and other dishes that pair well with alcohol.

Address: 1524 Sansom St, Philadelphia, PA 19102
Tel. No.: 215-972-9938

Royal Boucherie

Located at the Old City, Royal Boucherie is Chef Nick Elmi's collaboration with Philly bar royalty like Stephen Simmons and David Frank. A selection of house-made charcuterie and raw-bar offerings complements the main dishes and snacks that are graced with Elmi's French flair.

69

The two-level wood-and-leather dining room is graced by a fireplace, making Royal Boucherie an ideal location to share cocktails, a few hors d'oeuvres plates and a bottle of wine with natural notes. Essentially, the bar features an expertly-crafted ambience and menu offerings.

Address: 52 S 2nd St, Philadelphia, PA 19106
Web: royalboucherie.com
Tel. No.: 267-606-6313

Oloroso

If you ever want to enjoy a glass of sherry, head on over to Oloroso, a Spanish-style bar and restaurant that's located at Washington Square. Chef Townsend Wentz's menu for Oloroso is built around a tapas culture and is composed of boquerones, croquetas, and for-sharing paella pans.

A wine list, composed mostly of Spanish wines, is complemented with pours of various vermouths, bright Basque cider, and sherry varieties that you can choose from to pair with your food.

Oloroso has celebrated the value of sherry, which works as an aperitif or a cocktail modifier, and is being honored as a recipient of the 2018 Time Out Philadelphia Bar Awards as a result.

Address: 1121 Walnut St. Philadelphia, PA 19107
Web: olorosophilly.com
Tel. No.: 267-324-3014

Palizzi Social Club

Chef Joey Baladino has taken over his grandfather's South Philadelphia members-only social club and has transformed the place into a cozy Italian-American haven.

To maintain a family setting, only a handful of memberships are handed out every night at Palizzi Social Club.

Once you've entered this East Passyunk Crossing bar and club, you can enjoy any or more of its selection of wines and spirits, cocktails like negroni, and homemade dishes and desserts like spumoni, spaghetti with crabs, and stuffed artichokes.

Address: 1408 S 12th St, Philadelphia, PA 19147
Web: palizzisocial.com

12

Top 5 Night Clubs

Nightclubs and dance clubs have evolved since the days of flashing lights, pounding music, and garish attire. Some clubs held on to the age-old night club stereotypes while other clubs offer a relaxing atmosphere from the city noise with cocktails, plush seating, and perches from which to participate in the action.

Whether you're into Latin music or dig Top 40s music, there's always a place in Philadelphia where you can let loose, relax and enjoy a night out with coworkers, friends, or a romantic partner.

When you're in Philadelphia, you have the freedom to enjoy your night the way you want to. No matter where you want to end your day, there's always a place where you can enjoy great music, fantastic dancing, cocktails, and delicious hors d'oeuvres.

Zee Bar

Located at Penn's Landing, Zee Bar is an elegant way to wind down after a busy day trip. Start the evening with a crab and shrimp cocktail. You can try out other cocktails or enjoy a bottle service menu that lists sparkling wines like Dom and Cristal, and vodkas including Ketel One and Belvedere.

Performances by skilled acrobats add to the DJ lineup at the two-room Zee Bar, where applications for membership are taken at the entrance. The club opens Wednesdays to Saturdays and is open until 3:00am, so you'll never tire of its nightlife offerings.

Zee Bar offers dancing, drinks, various entertainment, excellent music, and an opportunity for you to meet up with friends.

Address: 100 Spring Garden Street Philadelphia, PA 19123
Web: zee-bar.com
Tel. No.: 215-922-2994

Tavern on Camac

Located at Center City, Tavern on Camac makes you feel like you're entering some historical building. However, what awaits you inside is far from the ordinary.

Tavern on Camac is a Gayborhood club that is one of gay nightlife and entertainment's main players. For those wanting to take a boogie break, listen to the Piano Bar show tunes that's played daily.

Show tunes are also featured at the 2nd-floor nightclub, Ascend, each Sunday, though karaoke, disco, DJs and a Ladies' night on Wednesday occupy the weekly calendar.

The welcoming Tavern on Camac is one of the city's least pretentious gay bars. The ground floor also has its Tavern Restaurant if you want a meal before enjoying the festivities upstairs. If you want to enjoy good food, excellent conversation, dancing, and upbeat music, spend your vacation nights at Tavern on Camac.

Address: 243 S Camac St, Philadelphia, PA 19107

Web: tavernoncamac.com
Tel. No.: 215-545-0900

The Roxxy

Located at Delaware Avenue in the Northern Liberties neigh-borhood, The Roxxy offers 4 rooms in which to dance to music as well as to party. The place can accommodate up to 2,000 partygoers and offers ample parking as well.

The bottle service is something you'd like to try, and you can also transfer from room to room if you want a change in scenery and pace. There's also a massive waterfront deck.

Come to The Roxxy if you enjoy bachelorette parties, serious parties, swimsuit competitions, and highly charged corporate events.

Address: 939 North Delaware AvenueGeneric, Philadelphia, PA 19123
Tel. No.: 484-388-1300

Brasil's

Located in the Old City, Brasil's has been churning out upbeat Latin tunes for over 15 years. Here, you can dance to tango, cha-cha, rhumba, and salsa tunes.

There are also nights when DJs take charge. Professional dance instructors also pop in for salsa classes on Wednesdays,

Fridays, and Saturdays. You can also book private dance lessons.

If you're serious about your Latin tunes, come to Brasil's and relax. Dancers from all experience levels come here to dance, and don't be shy if you're a beginner. Show your stuff and dance the night away.

Address: 112 Chestnut St, Philadelphia, PA 19106
Web: brasilsnightclub-philly.com
Tel. No.: 215-432-0031

Cuba Libre Restaurant & Rum Bar

At Cuba Libre Restaurant & Rum Bar, you feel like you're transported to that country a distance away from the Florida coast. Located at the Old City, this vibrant and fun club and restaurant features costumed dancers that lead partygoers into a spectacular floorshow.

This floorshow highlights singers, a Cuban master percussionist, and a Latin DJ spinning salsa, tropical dance, bachata, merengue, and Latin house tunes. After enjoying the show, the sangria- and mojito-drinking crowd gets to join the fun.

The bottle service offered includes spirits, including a 20+ year old rum that may tickle your senses. The Caribbean décor, tropical vibe, and Latin music make the Cuba Libre Restaurant & Rum Bar and excellent place to learn salsa or party with friends.

Address: 10 S. 2ND ST. Philadelphia

Web: http://cubalibrerestaurant.com/
en/philadelphia/
Tel. No.: 216-627-0666

13

Unique Things You Can Do Only in Philadelphia

You may know Philadelphia as the city where the Americans signed their Declaration for Independence. Political history aside, you'll discover that Philadelphia offers unique attractions that you can't do anywhere else in the world.

The city is rich with both the obscure and well-known history. Below are some of the activities you can enjoy only in the City of Brotherly Love.

Mummers

Every New Year's Day, the garishly-dressed mummers take center stage in Philadelphia, with their raucous, noisy parade at the heart of the city. The costume contest has since become legendary.

Mummers Parade

There's also a museum dedicated to them, the Mummers Museum. Here, you can see the best events throughout the mummers' history. You'll also know more about the mummers, who also had been around in ancient Greece. If ever you're in the city during the New Year, be sure to check out the mummers' parade.

Mummers Website : http://phillymummers.com/

Italian Market

The open-air Italian Market is the oldest of its kind in the country. There are many Italian markets over Philadelphia, but it's always a treat to be brought back in time to the early years of the Italian diaspora in the city.

At any time of the week, you can drop by this Italian Market and see a plethora of cheese, meat, fresh pasta, produce, or any other food item. Not only will you be enchanted by the sights, you'll also be delighted with the wonderful Italian aromas.

At around 11:00am during the yearly Italian Market Festival, you'll be entertained with live music and a tournament of half-ball, which is a street game that was popular in the city during the 1960s and 1970s.

Market Street 1911

Address: 919 S 9th St, Philadelphia
  Phone: +1 215-278-2903
  Italian Market Website
  https://italianmarketphilly.org/

Edgar Allan Poe House

The famed American author Edgar Allan Poe called this Northern Liberties structure his home for six years. Since being repurposed into a museum, Edgar Allan Poe's preserved abode is the best way for visitors to remember him as more than the author of The Pit and the Pendulum and The Raven.

For someone who had been considered emotionally disturbed, Edgar Allan Poe had an extraordinary body of work. His home has a basement that lent him inspiration for The Black Cat, a haunting and nostalgic short story.

Magic Gardens

The Magic Gardens was once a dilapidated structure, but it's now a symbol of the South Street revival. Over 14 years, Isaiah Zagar – a local mosaic artist – transformed the area into one of city's most unique art installations.

Magic Gardens

Magic Gardens is a wonderment of tunnels and found objects that now houses workshops, art classes, exhibitions, concerts, and many more. Magic Gardens is one of the few art installations that has seamlessly combined radical populism and artistic vision.

Magic Gardens

Magic Gardens Website : https://www.phillymagicgardens.org/

Reading Terminal Market

Whenever you happen to explore the outskirts of Philadel–

phia's Chinatown, you're likely to come across the packed Reading Terminal Market. This vibrant market is filled with restaurants and food stands that are not found anywhere else in the city.

Chinatown

Check out Bassett's Ice Cream and Beiler's Donuts. You can also visit the Market for locally-sourced cheese, meat, and produce. If you come here hungry, go to DiNic's and eat its much-hyped and acclaimed roast sandwich.

Address:51 N 12th St, Philadelphia
Phone:+1 215-922-2317

Reading Terminal Market Website
https://readingterminalmarket.org/

Schuylkill River Trail

A University City revitalization accomplishment is the first point of the Schuylkill River Trail. Once completed, the trail will run 130 miles (209km) up the Schuylkill River.

The trail's most urban parts, for now, have grand views of Boathouse Row as well as of the city's skyline. Farther down the trail, you can experience a nature walk or just bike through it.

Schuylkill River

Phone:+1 215-222-6030
Schuylkill River Trail Website
https://www.schuylkillbanks.org/

Historic Old City

Nothing reminds you of American Independence more than Philadelphia's Old City. Here, you'll find numerous vestiges of revolutionary history.

Liberty Bell

You'll find the Liberty Bell. Benjamin Franklin Museum and
the Betsy Ross House are your go-to places if you want to know

more about American history's funniest and oddest tidbits like the list of pseudonyms of Benjamin Franklin. You might even get to see an impressive Benjamin Franklin impersonator.

Philadelphia Downtown

14

Sample Three-Day Travel Itinerary

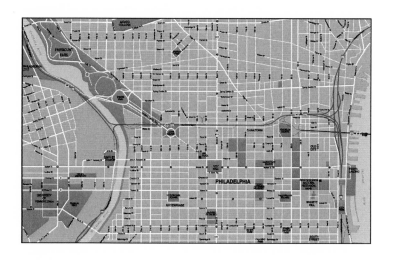

You can't tour Philadelphia in its entirety in just three days. However, you can tour the basics of this city within this period. Whether you're visiting friends or family in the city, you're on business, or you just want to explore the city, set aside time (three days, at least) to see Philly in a nutshell.

Some of the best places to start are at the vicinity of the Independence National Historical Park. When you have toured the park in its entirety, you can venture out and see some of the city's well-known museums as well as some of the local markets.

Below is a sample three-day travel itinerary that may inspire you. You can go to the places set in this itinerary or you can make your own. You can do a historical itinerary, a museum itinerary, or a culinary itinerary. The choice is yours.

Some tips to know on your Philly tour:

- Philadelphia is best experienced on foot, so make sure to bring along some comfy, sturdy shoes.
- The grid layout of Philadelphia allows you to easily navigate the urban areas.
- The trolley, subway, and bus service require exact change or tokens.
- Every 15 minutes, the Phlash shuttle runs from Penn's Landing to Philadelphia Museum. All-day and single-ride tickets are available.
- Tipping at restaurants is set at 15 to 20%.
- William Penn, in the 17th century, planned Philadelphia around five public squares: Franklin, City Hall, Rittenhouse,

Washington, and Logan. These squares are also excellent gathering spots.

Phlash Shuttle Website :https://www.ridephillyphlash.com/

Day 1

Reading Terminal Market

Established in 1892, Reading Terminal Market is composed of hawker shops and stalls from exotic meat, produce, flowers, and kitchenware. Here, you can eat a soft pretzel or be more adventurous and try raw oysters. Reading Terminal Market is located at 12th and Arch.

Duration: 1 to 2 Hours
Tips:
· Try DiNic's roast pork and broccoli rabe sandwich.
· Get one (or more) Beiler's Bakery sticky bun.

Elfreth's Alley

At 300 years old, Elfreth's Alley is the country's oldest residential street, and was the place where 18th century bakers, butchers, and artisans lived and worked.

Elfreth's Alley

Nowadays, you can find colorful shutters and flower boxes. The museum shares with visitors a glimpse into colonial life. Elfreth's Alley is at 124-126 Elfreth's Alley.

Duration: Less than one hour.

Tips:

- Visit the alley in the evening so you'll see the old lamps lighted up.
- The Museum is only open from April to September and operates Fridays to Sundays from 12:00pm to 5:00pm.
- Residents welcome the public to their homes twice yearly: in December (Deck the Alley) and in June (Fete Day).

Betsy Ross House

Betsy Ross is known for sewing the first American flag, which featured 13 stars and stripes to depict the first 13 states. The house is now a museum where you can see 18th century antiques. Betsy Ross House is located at 239 Arch St.

Betsy Ross House

Duration: Less than one hour.
   Tips:
   · Before coming here, stop by Benjamin Franklin's grave.
   · Get an audio tour.
   · Narrow staircases may discourage persons with disabilities from visiting.

95

United States Mint

The United States Mint was created in 1792, and the place still mints half of the country's circulating coins. The United States Mint is located at 151 N Independence Mall E.

United States Mint

Duration: Less than one hour.

Tips:

- Visit the gift shop, with its rare coin display.
- Admission is free.
- The Mint opens from Monday to Friday. It's also open on the Saturdays between Memorial Day and Labor Day.

National Constitution Center

The National Constitution Center displays historical government artifacts like Sandra Day O'Connor's judicial robe and a multimedia presentation of the country's constitutional history. The National Constitution Center is located at 525 Arch St Independence Mall.

Duration: 1 to 2 hours

Tips:

- Audio tours are an excellent supplement.
- There are special programs on civic holidays like Earth Day and Flag Day.
- The Museum's daily programs include a presidential trivia 'game show' and gallery talks.

Independence Hall

The Independence Hall is the country's birthplace. Here, you can see the Constitution's original draft as well as the

98

Declaration of Independence's first printing. Independence Hall is located at Chestnut St between 5th and 6th Streets.

Independence Hall

Duration: Less than one hour.

Tips:

- Tickets are often sold out. Thus, reserve tickets online or go early to the Visitor Center.
- Independence Hall opens daily from 9:00am to 5:00pm. From mid-May to early September, the place is open from 9:00am to 7:00pm.

Liberty Bell Pavilion

The 2,080-pound Liberty Bell used to hang at Independence Hall and rang for important events, most notably the Declaration of Independence's first public reading. Liberty Bell Pavilion is located at 6th St between Market and Chestnut Streets.

Duration: Less than one hour.
Tips:
- The famed 'crack' of the Bell is an attempt to fix a smaller split. You can even see drill bit marks if you look a bit closer.
- Check out the Bell's significance and history at the Liberty Bell Center before seeing the actual Bell up close.

Day 2

Parc Brasserie

This French bistro-style restaurant is lively and fun. During the warm months, you can enjoy a meal alfresco on the sidewalk that faces Rittenhouse Square.

Duration: 1 to 2 hours
Tip:
- You can get a table during the day even without reserving. However, you do need to get a dinner reservation as the place can be packed.

The Franklin Institute

The Franklin Institute is where you want to take your children to on your Philly vacation. Some interactive exhibits feature electricity experiments, simulated surfing, and a massive human heart for walkthroughs. The Franklin Institute is located at 222 N 20th St.

Duration: 1 to 2 hours

Tips:
- There are extra fees for some attractions and special exhibits.
- Purchase special exhibit tickets beforehand to guarantee your preferred time and date.

Eastern State Penitentiary

Eastern State Penitentiary was once known for keeping prisoners in solitary confinement, until overcrowding altered the circumstances. The prison reopened its doors in 1994 as a museum.

The decaying state only adds to the place's mystery and haunting beauty. Eastern State Penitentiary is located at 2124 Fairmount Avenue.

Duration: 1 to 2 hours

Tip:
- The audio guide, which is narrated by actor Steve Buscemi,

allows you to 'feel' the prison, and you're treated to sounds of a prison riot as well as of creaking doors.

Philadelphia Museum of Art

The Philadelphia Museum of Art houses a massive collection of American, Impressionist, Renaissance, and Modern art. The Museum is located at 2600 Benjamin Franklin Parkway.

Duration: 1 to 2 hours
Tips:
- From the Rocky Steps, you can glimpse the city's skyline.
- Admission prices include entry to the Rodin Museum, Perelman Building, Cedar Grove, and Mount Pleasant.

Day 3

Love Park
Officially called JFK Plaza, Love Park is where you can find the iconic 'LOVE' statue by Robert Indiana. The place is frequented by skateboarders, couples, and photography aficionados. Love Park is located at John F. Kennedy Blvd and North 15th St.

Duration: Less than one hour.

Tip:

- If possible, visit Love Park during non-peak hours as the place is a major photography spot.

Magic Gardens

In the 1960s, Isaiah Zagar and wife Julia began to beautify the neighborhood. However, it was only around 1994 that Zagar filled a lot with found objects and mosaics.

By 2002, the lot contained a maze of wine bottles, tiles and bicycle wheels. A non-profit now promotes and maintains Zagar's work. Magic Gardens is located at 1020 South St.

Duration: Less than one hour.

Tips:

- From April to October, you can join a neighborhood tour to learn more about Isaiah Zagar's work.
- The Museum opens daily, but at times opens late or closes early.
- The outside area may be closed during bad weather, but the staff may offer 'mini tours' each hour on the half hour.

Jim's Steaks South St.

Jim's Steaks South St is where you can get a unique Philly

cheesesteak eating experience. Before you enter the restaurant, you can smell the fragrant onions being cooked. The walls have pictures of celebrities who have visited. Jim's Steaks South St is located at 400 South St.

Duration: Less than one hour.

Tips:

- Be prepared to join the long lines of customers going to the restaurant.
- On weekends, Jim's is open late into the night.
- Cheese whiz is usually the choice cheese, but you can tell the cashier what cheese you prefer – whether you want provolone or American.

South Street

South Street is a famed city street that's packed with galleries, restaurants, shops, and nightlife destinations. Be sure to visit the stretch from Front to 10th Streets.

Duration: 1 to 2 hours

Tip:

- Ready your stomach. You'll be eating a lot along this tour.

Independence Seaport Museum

The Independence Seaport Museum focuses on the city's

port and seafaring industry. Children will love touring a real submarine and a ship. The Independence Seaport Museum is located at 211 S Columbus Blvd.

Duration: 1 to 2 hours
Tips:
- The Museum is not open on Sundays.
- Seafarin' Saturdays offer little sailors hands-on, fun activities. The events are held on Saturdays from 11:00am to 1:00pm.

15

Conclusion

I want to thank you for reading this book! I sincerely hope that you received value from it!

If you received value from this book, I want to ask you for a favour .Would you be kind enough to leave a review for this book on Amazon?

book are for clarifying purposes only and are the owned by the owners themselves, not affiliated with this document.

Made in United States
North Haven, CT
06 November 2021